PRESENT
MOMENT
WONDERFUL
MOMENT

OTHER BOOKS BY THICH NHAT HANH

PRESENT MOMENT WONDERFUL MOMENT

Mindfulness Verses
for Daily Living

THICH NHAT HANH

PARALLAX PRESS
BERKELEY, CALIFORNIA

Parallax Press
2236B Sixth Street
Berkeley, California 94710
parallax.org

Drawings copyright © 1993 Mayumi Oda
Cover design by Katie Eberle
Cover illustration by Jean-Marc Moschetti/encre-zen
Text design and composition by Maureen Forys
Printed on recycled paper

ISBN: 978-1-952692-22-2
Ebook ISBN: 978-1-952692-23-9

Library of Congress Control Number: 2022938289

2 3 4 5 VERSA 26 25 24 23

CONTENTS

VERSES FOR MEDITATION

VERSES FOR EATING MINDFULLY

FOREWORD
TO THE 2022 EDITION

AS MINDFULNESS IS BECOMING more mainstream, a question many of you may ask is: "How can mindfulness become an essential part of my daily life?"

In the depths of our human consciousness is the rhythm and cadence of poetry. We know that there are many levels of consciousness. Some levels use more effort and more energy while the deeper levels of consciousness use less energy. Our deepest insights arise from the depths of our consciousness where they may have been ripening for a very long time. Sometimes they arise in the form of a song or a poem, a phrase, or a sentence. Sometimes they go beyond words and can only be experienced in the depths of silence.

Gatha is a Sanskrit word meaning a verse of poetry. We use it in a very special sense in Plum Village to refer to short verses, usually of four lines. Gathas are the Thich Nhat Hanh poems that come from deep within the meditator. We entrust them to memory so that they can arise without effort as we go about our daily tasks in order to stay with what we are doing. They are a basic ingredient in the practice of mindfulness because they help us to be fully aware of what we are doing, so that our mind does not wander into the past or the future as we go about our daily activities. The second function of a gatha is to water positive, healing seeds in our consciousness, because a gatha will remind us of what is beautiful and wonderful in ourselves and around us.

You may already be familiar with the poetry of Dhyana Master Thich Nhat Hanh, and you know that he is a skilled poet. He has written more than 100 beautiful gathas to help us in our practice, some of which we wish to present in English here. As you become familiar with the practice of gathas, you may like to compose your own.

Our brain, our body, and our mind function depending on habit energy. In the beginning we have to apply our mind in order to learn a skill like cleaning our teeth. Soon the skill becomes a habit, and we brush our teeth without even being aware we are doing so. Our mind is occupied by things that have nothing to do with cleaning teeth. We are not present for life as it is here and now. The purpose of the verses in this book is to help you stay with the action you are doing in a positive and meaningful way. As you finish one action and begin another, you change from one verse to another.

During this time of Covid-19, many of you have joined us for online retreats. You have told us that because you have not been able to come to the practice center to enjoy a retreat led by the monks and nuns, you have been able to turn your home into a practice center or a monastery. For this reason, we should like to add some more verses that we practice in the monastery for you to use at home.

If you like, you can add a kind of journaling to your practice of gathas. You can make a list of the verses you practice every day. You can start with a couple of verses and then add more day by day. At the end of the day, you give yourself a certain number of stars depending on the quality of your practice of the verse in question.

	Sun	Mon	Tues	Weds	Thurs	Fri	Sat
Waking up	*	**	***	***	**	****	***
Brushing Teeth	*	**	***	****	***	****	***

This is how you can remind yourself to practice more diligently every day. Although you should memorize the verses, it is not just a matter of learning the words and repeating them. You need to feel something deeper as you remind yourself of the words. You need an experience of the effect of the words on your life.

In this new edition we have added some verses written by Thich Nhat Hanh some twenty years ago. Each of the verses begins with the words "In the historical dimension" or "In the ultimate dimension." These are the two dimensions in which we live our life. The historical dimension is marked by the limits of time and space and opposing ideas like same and different, you and I. The ultimate dimension takes us beyond these limited ideas. The ultimate dimension is always available for us to touch. The practice of using verses to accompany our daily actions in mindfulness has the function of taking us from the historical into the ultimate dimension. In our own time we need to be able to touch the ultimate dimension every day in order to nourish our spiritual life. We need to see how these two dimensions interpenetrate each other. What easier way than to use verses of poetry? We have a historical dimension that we need to live: to go to school, to go to work, to grow old. We can go to work every day as if it had nothing to do with our ultimate concern, going from one activity to the next as if we are on a treadmill. Or we can live our day at work deeply. It is up to us to choose whether we live the historical dimension deeply or like an automaton. When we live the historical dimension deeply, we are in touch with the ultimate dimension. In this dimension we can address our ultimate concerns: "What happens to us when we die? What is the purpose of life?" Life becomes a kaleidoscope of forms and colors closely interrelated to each other as we touch the ultimate dimension.

Sister Chan Duc

INTRODUCTION

EVERYONE HAS PAIN AND SUFFERING. IT is possible to let go of this pain and smile at our suffering. We can only do this if we know that the present moment is the only moment in which we can be alive. How wonderful to be alive!

Gathas are short verses that we can recite during our daily activities to help us return to the present moment and dwell in mindfulness. As exercises in both meditation and poetry, gathas are an essential part of Zen Buddhist tradition. Using a gatha doesn't require any special knowledge or religious practice. Some people like to memorize a favorite verse that they find they can come back to again and again. Others just like to write the verse down in a place they are likely to see it often.

The use of gathas goes back for over two thousand years. When I entered the Tu Hieu Monastery in Vietnam as a novice in 1942, I received a copy of *Gathas for Everyday Use,* compiled by the Chinese meditation master Du Ti. Du Ti's book of fifty gathas was written for monks and nuns of former times. At Plum Village, where I live in France, we practice gathas when we wake up, when we enter the meditation hall, during meals, and when we wash the dishes. In fact, we recite gathas silently throughout the entire day to help us attend to the present moment. One summer, to help the children and adults at Plum Village practice mindfulness, we began assembling gathas relevant for life today. The result is this book of practical, down-to-earth verses.

We often become so busy that we forget what we are doing or even who we are. I know people who say they even forget to breathe! We forget to look at the people we love and to appreciate them, until it is too late. Even when we have some leisure time, we don't know how to get in touch with what is going on inside and outside of ourselves. So we turn on the television or pick up the telephone as if we might be able to escape from ourselves.

To meditate is to be aware of what is going on—in our bodies, our feelings, our minds, and in the world. When we settle into the present moment, we can see beauties and wonders right before our eyes—a newborn baby, the sun rising in the sky. We can be very happy just by being aware of what is in front of us.

Reciting gathas is one way to help us dwell in the present moment. When we focus our mind on a gatha, we return to ourselves and become more aware of each action. When the gatha ends, we continue our activity with heightened awareness. When we drive a car, signs can help us find our way. The sign and the road become one, and we see the sign all along the way until the next sign. When we practice with gathas, the gathas and the rest of our life become one, and we live our entire lives in awareness. This helps us very much, and it helps others as well. We find that we have more peace, calm, and joy, which we can share with others.

As exercises in both meditation and poetry, gathas are a key part of the Zen tradition. When you memorize a gatha, it will come to you quite naturally when you are doing the related activity, be it turning on the water or drinking a cup of tea. You don't need to learn all the verses at once. You can find one or two that resonate with you and learn more over time. After some time, you may find that you have learned all of them and are even creating your own. When I wrote the gathas for using the telephone, driving a car, and turning on the computer, I did so within the tradition that I inherited from my teachers. You are now one of the inheritors of this tradition. Composing your own gathas to fit the specific circumstances of your life is one wonderful way to practice mindfulness.

I hope you find this collection of gathas a steady and delightful companion.

VERSES
FOR
STARTING
THE DAY

1

WAKING UP

Waking up this morning, I smile.
Twenty-four brand new hours are before me.
I vow to live fully in each moment
and to look at all beings with eyes of compassion.

What better way to start the day than with a smile? Your smile affirms your awareness and determination to live in peace and joy. How many days slip by in forgetfulness? What are you doing with your life? Look deeply, and smile. The source of a true smile is an awakened mind.

How can you remember to smile when you wake up? You might hang a reminder—such as a branch, a leaf, a painting, or some inspiring words—in your window or from the ceiling above your bed. Once you develop the practice of smiling, you may not need a sign. You will smile as soon as you hear a bird sing or see the sunlight stream through the window, and this will help you approach the day with more gentleness and understanding. The last line of this gatha comes from the Lotus Sutra.* The one who "looks at all beings with eyes of compassion" is Avalokiteshvara, the *bodhisattva* of compassion.

---

* See Thich Nhat Hanh, *Peaceful Action Open Heart: Lessons from the Lotus Sutra* (Berkeley, CA: Parallax Press, 2005).

In the sutra, this line reads: "Eyes of loving kindness look on all living beings." Love is impossible without understanding. To understand others, we must know them and be inside their skin. Then we can treat them with loving kindness. The source of love is our fully awakened mind.

2

STEPPING OUT OF BED

Morning, noon, eve, and night,
may all creatures take good care.
If I step on you by mistake,
may you transcend all fear.
Homage to the bodhisattva who transcends fear.

With this gatha we continue to water the seed of compassion in our heart. It can be recited right as we get out of bed and our feet touch the floor. Sitting on the edge of our bed, looking for our slippers, we remember this gatha. Every time we put on our shoes, we can also remember this gatha. We cultivate compassion for small insects, so when we meet them, we do not feel irritated with them. On the contrary we want to protect them. We see clearly that even the smallest insects experience fear of dying and want to live. The gift of non-fear is the greatest gift we can offer.

3

TAKING THE FIRST STEP OF THE DAY

Walking on the earth
is a miracle!
Each mindful step
reveals the wondrous Dharmakaya.

This poem can be recited as soon as we take the first step of the day. It can also be used during walking meditation or any time we stand up and walk.

Dharmakaya literally means the "body" (*kaya*) of the Buddha's teachings (*Dharma*), the way of understanding and love. It also is "the ground of being" manifested as mountains, rivers, stars, moon, and all species. Before passing away, the Buddha told his disciples, "Only my physical body will pass away. My Dharma body will remain with you forever." In Zen, the word has come to mean "the essence of all that exists." All phenomena—the song of a bird, the warm rays of the sun, a cup of hot tea— are manifestations of the Dharmakaya. We, too, are of the same nature as these wonders of the universe.

Walking on the earth is a miracle! We do not have to walk in space or on water to experience a miracle. The real miracle is to be awake in the present moment. Walking on the green earth, we realize the wonder of being alive. When we make steps like this, the sun of the Dharmakaya will shine.

4

TURNING ON THE LIGHT

Forgetfulness is the darkness;
mindfulness is the light.
I bring awareness
to shine upon all life.

When you touch a light switch, you can stop for a few seconds to recite this gatha before you turn on the light. Not only will there be light in the room, but there will also be light within you. Dwelling in the present moment is a miracle. Every illusion and random thought will disappear, just as darkness disappears when the light comes on. When we are mindful, we get in touch with the refreshing, peaceful, healing elements within ourselves and around us. Peace and joy are available at any time.

Conscious breathing helps us return to the present moment. I practice breathing every day. In my small meditation room, I have a calligraphy of the sentence, "Breathe, you are alive!" When mindfulness shines its light upon our activity, we recover ourselves and encounter life in the present moment. The present moment is a wonderful moment.

5

MAKING THE BED·

Making the bed with joy,
I tidy up my life.
As I guard body and mind,
bit by bit the afflictions end.

To guard body and mind means to be aware of what body and mind are doing and to keep them in the direction we have chosen for our life, the direction of understanding and love. Holding the blanket in our hands, we feel that matter and spirit are not two separate realities. We know that caring for our surroundings can bring peace into our lives.

6

OPENING THE WINDOW

Opening the window,
I look out onto the Dharmakaya.
How wondrous is life!
Attentive to each moment,
my mind is clear like a calm river.

After you wake up, you probably open the curtains and look outside. You may even like to open the window and feel the cool morning air with the dew still on the grass. But is what you see really "outside?" In fact, it is your own mind. As the sun sends its rays through the window, you are not just yourself. You are also the beautiful view from your window. You are all that exists; you are the Dharmakaya.

When we open the window and look out, we see that life is infinitely marvelous. At that very moment, we can vow to be awake all day long, realizing joy, peace, freedom, and harmony throughout our lives. When we do this, our mind becomes clear like a calm river.

7

TURNING ON THE WATER

Water flows from high mountain sources.
Water runs deep in the earth.
Miraculously, water comes to us
and sustains all life.

Even if we know the source of our water, we often take its appearance for granted. But it is thanks to water that life is possible. Our bodies are more than 70 percent water. Our food can be grown and raised because of water. Water is a good friend, a bodhisattva, that nourishes the many thousands of species on Earth. Its benefits are infinite.

Reciting this gatha before turning on the faucet or drinking a glass of water enables us to see the stream of fresh water in our own hearts so that we feel completely refreshed. To celebrate the gift of water is to cultivate awareness and help sustain our life and the lives of others.

8

WASHING YOUR FACE

Washing my face, I clean my mind.
Removing the dust,
the source of peace and joy
fills my whole body.

In the verse that the Master Shenxiu presented to the fifth patriarch of the Chinese Meditation school, it is said that the mind is a mirror, and every day we need to remove the dust from it. The very action of washing our face makes us feel good already, and we need to recognize that we are feeling good, otherwise we lose a precious opportunity of watering positive seeds. As we remove the dust from our face, we contemplate that we are removing the dust of afflictions from our mind, and gently remind ourselves to practice awareness of mind.

9

BRUSHING YOUR TEETH

Brushing my teeth and rinsing my mouth,
I vow to use truthful and loving speech.
When my mouth is fragrant with right speech,
a flower blooms in the garden of my heart.

Each toothpaste advertisement promises that this particular brand will make our mouth clean and our breath fragrant. But if we do not practice Right Speech, our breath can never be completely fragrant. In Vietnamese we say "Your words smell bad!" to mean "Your words are not kind or constructive, but rather they are sharp, slanderous, and misleading." Our speech can build a world of peace and joy in which trust and love can flourish, or it can create discord and hatred. Right Speech means that our words are both truthful and beautiful.

In 1964, several of us founded a new Buddhist order, the Order of Interbeing. The order developed fourteen mindfulness trainings. The ninth one reads:

> Aware that words can create happiness or suffering, we are committed to learning to speak truthfully, lovingly, and constructively. We will only use words that inspire joy, confidence, and hope as well as promote reconciliation and peace in ourselves and among people. We will speak and listen in a way that can help ourselves and others to

transform suffering and see the way out of difficult situations. We are determined not to say untruthful things for the sake of personal interest or to impress people, nor to utter words that might cause division or hatred. We will protect the joy and harmony of our Sangha by refraining from speaking about the faults of another person in their absence and always ask ourselves whether our perceptions are correct. We will speak only with the intention to understand and help transform the situation. We will not spread rumors nor criticize or condemn things of which we are not sure. We will do our best to speak out about situations of injustice, even when doing so may make difficulties for us or threaten our safety.

When we remember to speak words that are true, kind, and constructive, we nourish a beautiful flower in our heart, and we can offer its sweet fragrance to everyone.

10

RINSING YOUR MOUTH

Rinsing my mouth, my heart is cleansed.
The universe is perfumed with flowers.
When actions of body, speech, and mind are at peace,
the place where I am is at peace.

This gatha follows on the gatha for brushing our teeth. A pure land is not somewhere else. It is where the actions of body, speech and mind are at peace.

Often in daily life, our body and mind are separate. Sometimes our body is here, but our mind is lost in the past or focused on the future, possessed by anger, hatred, jealousy, or anxiety. If we can breathe mindfully, we bring mind and body together, and they become one again. This is what is meant by the expression "oneness of body and mind."

In rinsing our mouth, we can also take the time to clean and clear our hearts and minds. There is no separation.

11

LOOKING IN THE MIRROR

Awareness is a mirror
reflecting the four elements.
Beauty is a heart that generates love
and a mind that is open.

The moments during the day of looking in a mirror can be moments of deep awareness. The mirror can serve as a tool for cultivating mindfulness so that we develop a broad capacity to understand and love others. Anyone who maintains awareness in the present moment becomes beautiful and naturally emanates peace, joy, and happiness. A calm half smile and a loving heart are refreshing, and they allow miracles to unfold. The Buddha's smile is beautiful because it expresses tolerance, compassion, and loving kindness.

In the teachings of the Buddha, the four great elements are earth, water, fire, and air. The Vietnamese poet Tru Vu wrote:

The flower and its ephemeral fragrance
is made of the four elements.
Your eyes, shining with love,
are also made of the four elements

The four elements are neither mind nor matter. They are the universe itself revealed to us. When your mind is the clear mirror of meditative awareness, you will know that you are the outward expression of the essence of reality. So please smile. Smile with your eyes, not just with your lips. Smile with your whole being, reflecting the four elements in the mirror of mindful awareness.

12

USING THE TOILET

Defiled or immaculate,
increasing or decreasing—
these concepts exist only in our mind.
The reality of interbeing is unsurpassed.

Life is always changing. Each thing relies on every other thing for its very existence. If our mind is calm and clear, using the toilet can be as sacred as lighting incense. To accept life is to accept both birth and death, gain and loss, joy and sorrow, defilement and purity. The Heart Sutra teaches us that when we see things as they are, we do not discriminate between seeming opposites such as these.

Everything "inter-is." Understanding the truth of nonduality allows us to overcome all pain. Reciting this gatha can help us apply the teachings of the Heart Sutra, even during what is usually regarded as a mundane act.*

---

* For more on the Heart Sutra, see Thich Nhat Hanh, *The Other Shore* (Berkeley, CA: Parallax Press, 2017).

13

WASHING OUR HANDS

Water flows over these hands.
May I use them skillfully
to preserve our precious planet.

Our beautiful Earth is endangered. We are exhausting her resources and polluting her rivers, lakes, and oceans, destroying the habitats of many species, including our own. We are destroying the forests, the soil, the ozone layer, and the air. Because of our ignorance and fears, our planet may be destroyed as an environment that is hospitable to human life.

The earth stores water, and water gives life. Observe your hands as the water runs over them. Do you have enough clear insight to preserve and protect this beautiful planet, our Mother Earth?

14

BATHING

Unborn and indestructible,
beyond time and space—
Both transmission and inheritance
lie in the wonderful nature of the Dharmadhatu.

Whenever we take a bath or a shower, we can look at our body and see that it is a gift from our parents and their parents. Many of us in the West do not want to have much to do with our parents. They may have hurt us so much. But when we look deeply, we discover that it is impossible to drop all identity with them. As we wash each part of our body, we can meditate on the nature of the body and the nature of consciousness, asking ourselves, "To whom does this body belong? Who has transmitted this body to me? What has been transmitted?"

If we meditate in this way, we will discover that there are three components: the transmitter, that which is transmitted, and the one who receives the transmission. The transmitter is our parents. We are the continuation of our parents and their ancestors. The object of transmission is our body itself, and we are the one who receives the transmission. As we continue to meditate on this, we see clearly that the transmitter, the object transmitted, and the receiver are one. All three are present in our body.

When we are deeply in touch with the present moment, we can see that all our ancestors and all future generations are present in us. Seeing this, we will know what to do and what not to do—for ourselves, our ancestors, our children, and their children.

The Dharmadhatu is all that is manifested from the Dharmakaya, having Dharmakaya as its essence, just as all waves are manifestations of water. The Dharmadhatu is neither born nor destroyed. It has no previous existence and no future existence. Its existence is beyond time and space. When we understand this truth of existence with our whole being, we will begin to transcend the fear of death, and we will not be disturbed by unnecessary discriminations.

15

GETTING DRESSED

Putting on these clothes,
I am grateful to those who made them
and to the materials from which they were made.
I wish everyone could have enough to wear.

This gatha is an adaptation of a Vietnamese folk song: "My father works the land for the rice we eat. My mother sews the clothes I wear at every season." Today, not many of our fathers work the land; we buy our food in a store. Nor do many of our mothers sew our clothes; we buy manufactured clothes. By introducing the word "grateful," which is not in the folk song, the meaning becomes wider. In Zen monasteries, before eating, the monks reflect on the sources of their food. As we get dressed in the morning, we can contemplate the sources of our clothing and the fact that not everyone has enough to wear.

16

GREETING SOMEONE

A lotus for you,
a Buddha to be.

The tradition of joining our palms together and bowing when we meet someone is very beautiful. Millions of people in Asia and around the world greet each other this way every day. Forming a lotus bud with your hands is very pleasant. I hope you will try it from time to time. If a tulip blossom is more familiar for you to envision, you may want to say "A tulip for you, a Buddha to be." A tulip possesses the Buddha nature just like a lotus.

When someone offers me a cup of tea, I always bow respectfully. As I join my palms, I breathe in and say "A lotus for you." As I bow, I breathe out and say "A Buddha to be." To join our palms in a lotus bud is to offer the person standing before us a fresh flower. But we have to remember not to join our palms mechanically. We must be aware of the person we are greeting. When our respect is sincere, we remember that they have the nature of a Buddha, the nature of awakening.

If we look, we can see the Buddha in the person before us. When we practice this way regularly, we will see a change in ourselves. We will develop humility, and we will also realize that our abilities are boundless. When we know how to respect others, we also know how to respect ourselves.

As I bow, mindfulness becomes real in me. Seeing my deep reverence, the person to whom I bow also becomes awake, and he may like to form a lotus and bow to me, breathing in and out. With one greeting, mindfulness becomes present in both of us as we touch the Buddha with our hearts, not just with our hands. Suddenly, the Buddha in each of us begins to shine, and we are in touch with the present moment.

Sometimes we think that we are superior to others—perhaps more educated or intelligent. Seeing an uneducated person, a feeling of disdain may arise, but this attitude does not help anyone. Our knowledge is relative and limited. An orchid, for example, knows how to produce noble, symmetrical flowers, and a snail knows how to make a beautiful, well-proportioned shell. Compared with this kind of knowledge, our knowledge is not worth boasting about, no matter how much formal education we have. We should bow deeply before the orchid and the snail and join our palms reverently before the monarch butterfly and the magnolia tree. Feeling respect for all species of living beings and inanimate objects will help us recognize a part of the Buddha nature in ourselves.

VERSES
FOR
MEDITATION

17

FOLLOWING THE BREATH

Breathing in, I calm my body.
Breathing out, I smile.
Dwelling in the present moment,
I know this is a wonderful moment.

In our very busy society, it is a great fortune to be able to breathe consciously from time to time. Our body and mind become calm and concentrated, bringing us joy, peace, and ease. We can breathe consciously while sitting in meditation or at any time throughout the day. Any time we are aware of our breathing, we can recite this gatha.

"Breathing in, I calm my body." This line is like drinking a glass of cold water. You feel the cool freshness permeating your body. When I breathe in and recite this line, I actually feel the breathing calming my body and mind. "Breathing out, I smile." A smile can relax hundreds of muscles in your face and make you master of yourself. That is why the Buddhas and bodhisattvas are always smiling.

"Dwelling in the present moment." While I sit here, I don't think of anything else. I sit here, and I know where I am. "I know this is a wonderful moment." It is a joy to sit, stable and at ease, and return to ourselves—our breathing, our half smile, our true nature. We can appreciate these moments. We can ask ourselves, "If I do not have peace and joy right now, when will I have peace and joy—tomorrow or after tomorrow? What is preventing me from being happy right now?" When we follow our breathing, we can say, "Calming, smiling, present moment, wonderful moment."

This exercise is for both beginners and experienced practitioners. Many of us who have practiced for forty or fifty years continue to practice in the same way, because it is so vital. In the Sutra on the Full Awareness of Breathing, the Buddha proposed sixteen exercises to help us breathe consciously.* This gatha is a condensation of many of these exercises. Another condensation is this verse:

> *Breathing in, I know I'm breathing in.*
> *Breathing out, I know I'm breathing out.*
> *As the in-breath grows deep, the out-breath grows slow.*
> *Breathing in makes me calm. Breathing out brings*
> *   me ease.*
> *With the in-breath, I smile. With the out-breath,*
> *   I release.*
> *Breathing in, there is only the present moment.*
> *Breathing out, it is a wonderful moment.*

* For the complete sutra and commentary, see Thich Nhat Hanh, *Breathe, You are Alive!: The Sutra on the Full Awareness of Breathing* (Berkeley, CA: Parallax Press, 1996, 2008).

The verse can be summarized in these eight words and two phrases:

In, Out.
Deep, Slow.
Calm, Ease.
Smile, Release.
Present moment, Wonderful moment.

This is very easy to practice—while sitting, walking, standing, or doing any activity.

First, we practice "In, Out." Breathing in, we say "In" silently, to nourish the awareness that we are breathing in. When we breathe out, we say "Out," aware that we are breathing out. Each word is a guide to help us return to our breathing in the present moment. We can repeat "In, Out" until we find that our concentration is peaceful and solid. Most important is that we enjoy doing it.

Then we say "Deep" with the next inhalation, and "Slow" with our exhalation. When we breathe consciously, our breathing becomes deeper and slower. We do not have to make a special effort but only notice that it is deeper and slower, more peaceful and pleasant. We can continue to breathe with the phrase "Deep, Slow, Deep, Slow" until we want to move to the next phrase, which is "Calm, Ease."

The word "Calm" comes from the exercise in the sutra: "I am breathing in and making the activities of my whole body calm and at peace. I am breathing out and making the activities of my whole body calm and at peace." The word "body" here also means "mind" because during the practice body and mind become one.

When we breathe out, we say, "Ease." Ease means a feeling of not being pressured, feeling free. Our time is only for breathing and enjoying breathing. We feel light and free, at ease. We know that breathing is the most important thing at this moment, so we just enjoy the practice of breathing. The feeling of ease is one of the seven factors of enlightenment in Buddhism.

When we have mastered "Calm, Ease," we move to "Smile, Release." When we breathe in, even if we do not feel great joy at that moment, we can still smile. But in fact, it is unlikely because after practicing breathing in this way, we already have joy and peace. When we smile, our joy and peace become even more settled, and tension vanishes. It's a kind of "mouth yoga." We smile for everyone.

When we breathe out, we say "Release."

18

MORNING MEDITATION

The Dharmakaya is bringing morning light.
Sitting still, my heart is at peace.
I smile.
This is a new day.
I vow to go through it in awareness.
The sun of wisdom will shine everywhere.

If we have mindfulness and concentration, everything we see and hear in our daily life becomes a Dharma talk—a falling leaf, a flower as it opens, a bird flying by, the sound of a bird calling. We say that it is the Dharmakaya, the Dharma body of the Buddha, which is always revealing the teaching of the Dharma.

When we are refreshed and attentive, we can be in touch with the Dharma body and hear the Dharma being taught from moment to moment. We shall see that it's not necessary to play a CD or go online in order to hear the Dharma. We can hear the Dharma at any moment.

19

PLACING YOUR SHOES

Placing my shoes neatly,
may everyone's steps
always be mindful,
coming in and going out in freedom.

"Coming in and going out in freedom" can refer to our everyday movements going in and out of a building or a room. It can also refer to our birth and death. Birth and death are seen as doors through which we go in and out. We aspire that we ourselves and others be free of the bonds of birth and death so we can die in freedom and transition in freedom to our next manifestation.

20

ENTERING THE
MEDITATION ROOM

Entering the meditation room,
I see my true self.
As I sit down,
I vow to cut off all disturbances.

I think it would be a good idea if each household had a "breathing room." We have so many rooms—for sleeping, eating, and so forth. Why not a room for breathing? Each time we need to return to ourselves, we can go into this simple room and sit quietly, following our breathing. Conscious breathing is very important. Even if you don't have room for a whole separate space, wherever you find a quiet place to breathe and meditate for a few moments, that is your meditation room.

In the Vietnamese version of this gatha, the word for "disturbances" is *tram luan.* It means "sinking into and rolling in the ocean of forgetfulness, worries, and afflictions." Stepping into the meditation room, we can remember our desire for complete liberation. By dwelling in the present moment, our steps can establish total freedom so that peace and equanimity are available at once.

21

LIGHTING A CANDLE

Lighting this candle,
offering the light to countless Buddhas,
the peace and joy I feel
brighten the face of the earth.

In many Asian countries, people make offerings to the figures on the altar or shrine. We usually have a candle, some flowers, a bowl of fruit, and a stick of incense. As we light the candle mindfully, the veils of ignorance and forgetfulness naturally dissolve, and the earth herself becomes filled with light.

There is a story in the life of the Buddha that describes how profound an offering of light can be. One day, the people of the city of Shravasti honored the Buddha by lighting thousands of lamps around the Jetavana monastery. An old mendicant woman wanted to make an offering, but after a whole day of begging, she only had one cent. So she bought some oil with that penny and poured it into one of the lamps.

The next morning, the Venerable Mahamaudga-lyayana went outside to blow out the lamps. All the lamps went out except the one with the oil poured by the beggar woman. The harder he tried to blow out that light, the brighter it grew. A candle offered in mindfulness is like the light the old beggar woman offered to the Buddha many years ago.

Although this gatha was composed for lighting a candle in a meditation hall, it can be used when we light candles anywhere, such as during a vigil for human rights or during a storm. It can even be used for turning on an electric light.

22

OFFERING INCENSE

In gratitude, we offer this incense
to all Buddhas and bodhisattvas
throughout space and time.
May it be fragrant as Earth herself,
reflecting our careful efforts,
our wholehearted awareness,
and the fruit of understanding, slowly ripening.
May we and all beings be companions
of Buddhas and bodhisattvas.
May we awaken from forgetfulness
and realize our true home.

In Vietnamese Zen temples, we say this gatha silently as we offer incense alone, or aloud when we conduct ceremonies with others. As we say it, we imagine fragrant smoke rising in the air, becoming a cloud of five colors. This represents the offering to all Buddhas throughout space and time, of the fivefold fragrance: precepts, concentration, understanding, liberation, and insight. We call it the "fragrance of the heart," a delight that is available to us every day, although not for sale in stores. When we offer incense, we vow with all beings to leave the world of forgetfulness and return to the world of awakening. Forgetfulness is the lack of mindfulness. Awakening is true freedom.

23

PRAISING THE BUDDHA

As refreshing as a lotus flower,
as bright as the North Star,
to the Buddha
I go for refuge.

In Zen Buddhism, we join our palms together before the image of the Buddha, our teacher, and praise his beauty, which is the fruit of love and understanding. Lotus flowers are fresh and pure, and they can be compared with love. The North Star helps travelers find their direction, so it symbolizes understanding. To take refuge in the Buddha is to seek protection in understanding, loving kindness, and compassion.

In Buddhism, there are three places where a person can go for protection and shelter: the Buddha, the Dharma (the teachings of the Buddha), and the Sangha (our friends who guide us and support us in our spiritual journey). Buddhism calls these three refuges the Three Jewels because they are our spiritual wealth, our inheritance; we always have these three places of support and protection.

24

SITTING DOWN

Sitting here is like sitting under
the Bodhi tree.
My body is mindfulness itself,
calm and at ease,
free from all distraction.

The Buddha realized complete awakening after sitting at the foot of a *ficus religiosa*, now called a bodhi tree. "Bodhi" means to be awake or liberated. The word for liberation in Sanskrit is *vimukti*. Today, the place where Buddha realized awakening is called Bodh Gaya, and a large temple has been built there to commemorate his awakening. The bodhi tree stands, beautiful with its luxuriant growth—a grandchild of the tree which stood there in the Buddha's time.

When we arrive at our meditation cushion or chair, we can join our palms, make a small bow from the waist, and recite this verse. Then we sit down slowly and carefully. When we sit on our cushion with the intention of realizing full awareness of the present moment, our sitting is the continuation of the Buddha's awakened mind. Meditation is not passive sitting in silence. It is sitting in awareness, free from distraction, and realizing the clear understanding that arises from concentration.

25

INVITING THE BELL

Body, speech, and mind in perfect oneness—
I send my heart along with the sound of the bell.
May the hearers awaken from forgetfulness
and transcend all anxiety and sorrow.

In Buddhist meditation centers, we often use bowl-shaped bells to punctuate the day, calling the community to mindfulness. Standing or sitting in front of the bell, we join our palms, breathe three times, and recite this verse. We hold the bell "inviter" (a wooden stick) in one hand, and the bell, if it is small enough, in the palm of the other, concentrating on the position of our hand and the stick. First, we "wake up the bell" by touching its rim lightly with the inviter. This brief sound tells everyone that a full sound of the bell will come in a moment.

During retreats, the sound of the bell reminds us to return to our breathing in the present moment. When we hear it, we stop talking and thinking and breathe consciously three times. It is important that the person who invites the bell to sound quiets their own being first. If their body, speech, and mind are quiet and in harmony when they invite the bell, the sound will be solid, beautiful, and joyful, and this will help the hearers wake up to the present moment and overcome all anxiety and sorrow.

26

LISTENING TO THE BELL

May the sound of this bell
penetrate deeply into the cosmos.
In even the darkest places,
may living beings hear it clearly
so that understanding may light up their hearts
and, without hardship, they may transcend
the realms of birth and death.

The work of meditation is to awaken us to birth and death; then birth and death can never touch us. In the historical dimension we have birth certificates and death certificates; this is the world of waves. A wave has its beginning and end, but we cannot ascribe these characteristics to water. In the world of water, there is no birth or death, no being or nonbeing, no beginning or end. When we touch the water, we touch reality in its ultimate dimension and are liberated from all of those concepts.

A flower contains the whole of the cosmos. It is born from soil, minerals, seeds, sunshine, rain, and many other things. Meditation reveals to us the interbeing, no-birth no-death nature of all things. Life is a continuation. The dry leaf falls to earth and becomes part of the moist soil, preparing to appear on the tree the following spring in another form. Everything is pretending to be born and pretending to die. The day of our so-called death is a day of our continuation in many other forms. If you know how to touch your loved ones in the ultimate dimension, they will always be with you even after they have passed away. If you look very deeply, you can see them smiling to you.

27

LETTING GO

Hearing the bell,
I am able to let go of all afflictions.
My heart is calm,
my sorrows ended.
I am no longer bound to anything.
I learn to listen to my suffering
and the suffering of the other person.
When understanding is born in me,
compassion is also born.

Every day there are ways in which we get caught in attachments, and so we continue to suffer. If only we could learn the art of releasing, happiness would come right away. Our worries and concerns prevent us from getting in touch with the wonders of life. We have all had the experience of being reminded of what is most important to us. Sometimes we are reminded by a friend or a teacher. Sometimes it may be the sound of the bell, bringing us back to ourselves in the present moment, enabling us to see the situation more clearly. Then we can let go of our worry, craving, or concern, so we can be free to encounter the wonders of life that are always there in the here and the now.

We are also free to be able to see the suffering in another person. If we follow our breathing and observe someone mindfully, we can be in contact with their suffering, and the energy of compassion arises in us. As their physical and psychological suffering becomes clear, the mind of compassion arises based on our understanding. Compassion and understanding give rise to each other and depend on each other.

Our thoughts and actions should express our mind of compassion, even when the other person says and does things that are not easy to accept. We practice like this until we see clearly that our love does not depend on the other person apologizing or being lovable. Then we can know that our mind of compassion is firm and authentic.

28

ADJUSTING YOUR POSTURE

Feelings come and go
like clouds in a windy sky.
Conscious breathing
is my anchor.

If your legs or feet fall asleep or begin to hurt during sitting meditation so that your concentration becomes disturbed, feel free to adjust your position. If the pain is severe, stand up, walk slowly and mindfully, and then when you are ready, sit down again.

According to the Abhidharma texts of Buddhist psychology, there are three kinds of feelings—pleasant, unpleasant, and neutral. This way of dividing feelings doesn't seem accurate, because when there is full awareness, neutral feelings can become pleasant feelings which are more sound and longer lasting than other kinds of pleasant feelings.

To eat good food or hear words of praise usually gives rise to a pleasant feeling. Flying into a rage or having a toothache is an unpleasant feeling. These feelings usually push us around, and we become like clouds blown in the wind. Our feelings of peace and joy will be more stable and lasting if we know the source of our so-called neutral feelings. The essence of happiness is a body that is not in pain and a heart and mind that are not oppressed by anxiety, fear, or hatred. Sitting in meditation, we can arrive at a stable feeling of joy, realizing the stillness of body and the clarity of mind. We are no longer pushed around by these "roots of affliction," and we experience a feeling of well-being.

Sitting meditation is to establish stillness, peace, and joy. Just as an anchor holds a boat so that it does not drift away, conscious breathing sustains our awareness of the present moment and keeps us in touch with our true selves. The necessary condition for the existence of peace and joy is the awareness that peace and joy are available.

29

CLEANING THE
MEDITATION ROOM

As I clean
this fresh, calm room,
boundless joy
and energy arise!

It is a joy to tidy the meditation room. In its fresh, calm atmosphere, everything reminds us to come back to the present moment. Every sweep of the broom is light, and every step we take is filled with awareness. As we arrange the cushions, our mind is still. Working in a relaxed way, with a feeling of peace and joy, we become energized. Everything we do can be filled with this peace and joy.

30

WALKING MEDITATION

The mind can go in a thousand directions,
but on this beautiful path, I walk in peace.
With each step, a gentle wind blows.
With each step, a flower blooms.

The purpose of walking meditation is really to enjoy the walking—walking not in order to arrive, but in order to walk. The purpose is to be in the present moment and enjoy each step you make. Therefore, you have to shake off all worries and anxieties, not thinking of the future, not thinking of the past, just enjoying the present moment. You can take the hand of a child as you walk, as if you are the happiest person on Earth. We walk all the time, but usually it is more like running. Our hurried steps print anxiety and sorrow on the earth. If we can take one step in peace, we can take two, three, four, and then five steps for the peace and happiness of humankind.

Our mind darts from one thing to another, like a monkey swinging from branch to branch without stopping to rest. Thoughts have millions of pathways, and we are forever pulled along by them into the world of forgetfulness. If we can transform our walking path into a field for meditation, our feet will take every step in full awareness. Our breathing will be in harmony with our steps, and our mind will naturally be at ease. Every step we take will reinforce our peace and joy and cause a stream of calm energy to flow through us. Then we can say, "With each step, a gentle wind blows."

The Buddha is often represented by artists as seated upon a lotus flower to suggest the peace and happiness he enjoys. Artists also depict lotus flowers blooming under the footsteps of the newly born Buddha. If we take steps without anxiety, in peace and joy, then we too will cause a flower to bloom on the earth with every step.

VERSES
FOR
EATING
MINDFULLY

31

WASHING VEGETABLES

In these fresh vegetables
I see a green sun.
All dharmas join together
to make life possible.

The first two lines are taken from my poem "Armfuls of Poetry and Bushels of Sunshine."*

In fact, it is the sun that is green and not just the vegetables, because the green color of the leaves would not be possible without the presence of the sun. Without the sun, no species of living being could survive. Leaves absorb sunlight as it is reflected on their surfaces, and they retain the energy of the sun, extracting the carbon in the atmosphere that manufactures the nutritive matter necessary for the plant.

Therefore, when we see fresh vegetables, we can see the sun in them—a sun green in color—and not just the sun, but thousands of other phenomena as well. For example, if there were no clouds there would be no rainwater. Without water, air, and soil, there would be no vegetables.

* See Thich Nhat Hanh, *Call Me By My True Names* (Berkeley, CA: Parallax Press, 1999).

The vegetables are the coming together of many conditions far and near.

In the gatha, the word "dharmas" means phenomena. In everyday life, whenever you are in contact with any phenomenon whatsoever, you can always engage in the practice of meditation on interdependent origination, not just when you are washing vegetables. The Sanskrit word *pratitya-samutpada,* usually translated as "codependent origination," means that phenomena exist in relationship to all other things. All dharmas join together, making life possible.

32

LOOKING AT
YOUR EMPTY BOWL

My bowl, empty now,
will soon be filled with precious food.
Beings all over the earth are struggling to live.
How fortunate we are to have enough to eat.

When many people on this earth look at an empty bowl, they know their bowl will continue to be empty for a long time. So the empty bowl is as important to honor as the full bowl. We are grateful to have food to eat, and with this gatha, we can vow to find ways to help those who are hungry.

33

SERVING FOOD

In this food
I see clearly
the presence of the entire universe
supporting my existence.

This verse helps us see the principle of dependent co-arising, as we see that our life and the lives of all species are interrelated. Eating is a very deep practice. As you wait to serve yourself or be served, look at the food and smile to it. Each morsel of food is an ambassador from the cosmos. It contains sunshine, clouds, the sky, the earth, the farmer, everything. Each morsel of food is a piece of bread offered to you by the Buddha.

Look into the bread, the carrot, and touch it deeply. When you are eating your meal, pick up one piece of carrot, and don't put it into your mouth right away. Look at it and smile to it, and if you are mindful, you will see deeply into the piece of carrot; sunshine is inside, a cloud is inside, the great earth is inside, a lot of love and a lot of hard work is inside. When you have seen clearly the real piece of carrot, put it into your mouth and chew it in mindfulness. Please be sure to chew only carrots, and not your projects or your worries. Enjoy chewing your carrot. The piece of carrot is a miracle. You, also, are a miracle.

So spend time with your food; every minute of your meal should be happy. Not many people have the time and the opportunity to sit down and enjoy a meal like that. We are very fortunate.

34

LOOKING AT YOUR PLATE

This plate of food,
so fragrant and appetizing,
also contains much suffering.

This gatha has its roots in a Vietnamese folksong. When we look at our plate, filled with fragrant and appetizing food, we should be aware of the bitter pain of people who suffer from hunger. Every day, thousands of children die from hunger and malnutrition. Looking at our plate, we can see Mother Earth, the farmworkers, and the tragedy of the unequal distribution of food.

We who live in North America and Europe are accustomed to eating foods imported from other countries, whether it is coffee from Colombia, chocolate from Ghana, or fragrant rice from Thailand. Many children in these countries, except those from rich families, never see the fine products that are put aside for export in order to bring in money. Some parents are so poor and starving, they have to sell their children as servants to families who have enough to eat.

Before a meal, we can join our palms in mindfulness and think about those who do not have enough to eat. Slowly and mindfully, we breathe three times and recite this gatha. Doing so will help us maintain mindfulness.

May we find ways to live more simply in order to have more time and energy to change the system of injustice that exists in the world.

35

THE FIVE CONTEMPLATIONS

This food is the gift of the earth, the sky, numerous living beings, and much hard and loving work.

May we eat with mindfulness and gratitude so as to be worthy to receive this food.

May we recognize and transform unwholesome mental formations, especially our greed, and learn to eat with moderation.

May we keep our compassion alive by eating in such a way that reduces the suffering of living beings, stops contributing to climate change, and heals and preserves our precious planet.

We accept this food so that we may nourish our brotherhood and sisterhood, build our Sangha, and realize our ideal of serving all living beings.

The first contemplation is being aware that our food comes directly from the earth and sky. It is a gift of the earth and sky, and also of the people who prepared it.

The second contemplation is about being worthy of the food we eat. The way to be worthy of our food is to eat mindfully—to be aware of its presence and thankful for having it. We cannot allow ourselves to get lost in our worries, fears, or anger over the past or the future. We are there for the food because the food is there for us; it is only fair. Eat in mindfulness and you will be worthy of the earth and the sky.

The third contemplation is about becoming aware of our negative tendencies and not allowing them to carry us away. We need to learn how to eat in moderation, to eat the right amount of food. The bowl that is used by a monk or a nun is referred to as an "instrument of appropriate measure." It is very important not to overeat. If you eat slowly and chew very carefully, you will get plenty of nutrition. The right amount of food is the amount that helps us stay healthy.

The fourth contemplation is about our way of eating and producing food, which can be very violent to other species, to our own bodies, and to the earth. Our way of growing, distributing, and eating food can be part of creating a larger healing. With each meal, we get to choose.

The fifth contemplation is being aware that we receive food in order to realize something. Our lives should have meaning and that meaning is to help people suffer less, to help them to touch the joys of life. When we have compassion in our hearts and when we know that we are able to help a person suffer less, life begins to have more meaning. This is very important food for us and can bring us a lot of joy. A single person is capable of helping many living beings. And it is something we can do anywhere.

36

BEGINNING TO EAT

With the first mouthful, I practice the love that brings joy.
With the second mouthful, I practice the love that relieves
*   suffering.*
With the third mouthful, I practice the joy of being alive.
With the fourth mouthful, I practice equal love for all
*   beings.*

This verse refers to Buddhism's Four Immeasurable Minds (*brahmavihara* in Sanskrit)—loving kindness, compassion, joy, and inclusiveness. These are said to be the four homes of the Buddhas and bodhisattvas. During the time we eat the first mouthful, we may like to express our gratitude by promising to bring joy to at least one person. With the second mouthful, we can promise to help relieve the pain of at least one person. With the third mouthful, we are in touch with the wonders of life. With the fourth mouthful, we practice inclusiveness and the love that is characterized by nondiscrimination. After this, we get in touch with the food and its deep nature.

Eating can be very joyful. When I pick up my food, I take time to look at it for a moment before I put it in my mouth. If I am really present, I will recognize the food right away, whether it is a carrot, a string bean, or a piece of bread. I smile to it, put it in my mouth, and chew with complete awareness of what I am eating—mindfulness is always mindfulness *of* something—and I chew my food in such a way that life, joy, solidity, and non-fear become possible. After twenty minutes of eating, I feel nourished, not only physically but also mentally and spiritually. This is a very deep practice.

37

FINISHING YOUR MEAL

My bowl is empty.
My hunger is satisfied.
I vow to live
for the benefit of all beings.

After we have eaten, we don't need to rush on to the next thing. Instead, we can spend a moment being grateful for the food we have just eaten and all that was necessary to create this moment. This verse reminds us of the Four Gratitudes: to our parents who give us life, our teachers who show us the way, our friends who support us on the path and help us in difficult moments, and all organic and inorganic species—plants, animals, and minerals—that nourish and enrich our lives.

Sometimes we show our gratitude before we eat and then move on. But we are as grateful for fullness as we are for the moment before we eat. Living peacefully and happily is the best way to show our gratitude and is our greatest gift for the world and the next generation. How we eat can model so much to those around us. Our children need our happiness, not our money. If we know how to live happily with each other, the children will learn it from us. That is the greatest inheritance we can hand down to our children.

38

WASHING THE DISHES

Washing the dishes
is like bathing a baby Buddha.
The profane is the sacred.
Everyday mind is Buddha mind.

The idea that doing dishes is unpleasant can occur to us only when we are not doing them. Once we are standing in front of the sink with our sleeves rolled up and our hands in warm water, it is really not bad at all. I enjoy taking my time with each dish, being fully aware of the dish, the water, and each movement of my hands. I know that if I hurry in order to go and have dessert, the time will be unpleasant. That would be a pity, for the dishes themselves and the fact that I am here washing them are both miracles!

Each thought, each action in the sunlight of awareness becomes sacred. In this light, no boundary exists between the sacred and the profane. It may take a bit longer to do the dishes, but we can live fully, happily, in every moment. Washing the dishes is at the same time a means and an end—that is, not only do we do the dishes in order to have clean dishes, we also do the dishes just to do the dishes and live fully each moment while washing them.

If I am incapable of washing dishes joyfully, if I want to finish them quickly so I can go and have dessert and a cup of tea, I will be equally incapable of doing these other things joyfully. With the cup in my hands, I will be thinking about what to do next, and the fragrance and flavor of the tea, together with the pleasure of drinking it, will be lost. I will always be dragged into the future, never able to live in the present moment. The time of dishwashing is as important as the time of sitting or walking meditation. That is why the everyday mind is called Buddha mind.

39

DRINKING TEA

This cup of tea in my two hands,
mindfulness held perfectly.
My mind and body dwell
in the very here and now.

Wherever you are drinking your tea, whether at work or in a café or at home, it is wonderful to allow enough time to appreciate it. You can hold a cup of tea in your two hands, breathe consciously, and say the above gatha either out loud or to yourself. If the weather is cold, you can feel the warmth of the cup in your hands. Breathe in and recite the first line, breathe out and recite the second. The next inhalation is for the third line, and the next exhalation is for the fourth. Breathing mindfully in this way, we recuperate ourselves, and the cup of tea reclaims its highest place. If we are not mindful, it is not tea that we are drinking but our own illusions and afflictions.

When our mind and body have become one and we are awake, we are ourselves and we can encounter the tea. If the tea becomes real, we become real. When we are able to truly meet the tea, at that very moment, we are alive. As we drink the tea, we are well aware that we are drinking the tea. Drinking tea becomes the most important thing in life at that moment. This is the practice of mindfulness.

NOTES ON EATING MINDFULLY

A few years ago, I asked some children, "What is the purpose of eating breakfast?" One boy replied, "To get energy for the day." Another said, "The purpose of eating breakfast is to eat breakfast." I think the second child is more correct. The purpose of eating is to eat.

Eating a meal in mindfulness is an important practice. We turn off the TV, put down our newspaper, and work together for five or ten minutes, setting the table and finishing whatever needs to be done. During these few minutes, we can be very happy. When the food is on the table and everyone is seated (remember the gatha for sitting down), we practice breathing: "Breathing in, I calm my body. Breathing out, I smile," three times. We can recover ourselves completely after three breaths like this. Then, we look at each person as we breathe in and out in order to be in touch with ourselves and everyone at the table. We don't need two hours in order to see another person. If we are really settled within ourselves, we only need to look for one or two seconds, and that is enough to see our friend. I think that if a family has five members, only about five or ten seconds is needed to practice this "looking and seeing."

After breathing, we smile. Sitting at the table with other people, we have a chance to offer an authentic smile of friendship and understanding. It is very easy, but not many people do it. To me, this is the most important practice. We look at each person and smile to them. Breathing and smiling together are very important practices. If the people in a family cannot smile to each other, the situation is a very dangerous one.

After breathing and smiling, we look down at the food in a way that allows the food to become real. This food reveals our connection with the earth. Each bite contains the life of the sun and the earth. The extent to which our food reveals itself depends on us. We can see and taste the whole universe in a piece of bread! Contemplating our food for a few seconds before eating, and eating in mindfulness, can bring us much happiness.

Having the opportunity to sit with our family and friends and enjoy wonderful food is something precious, something not everyone has. Many people in the world are hungry. When I hold a bowl of rice or a piece of bread, I know that I am fortunate, and I feel compassion for all those who have no food to eat and are without friends or family. This is a very deep practice. We do not need to go to a temple or a church to practice this. We can practice it right at our dinner table. Mindful eating can cultivate seeds of compassion and understanding that will strengthen us to do something to help hungry and lonely people be nourished.

In order to aid mindfulness during meals, you may like to eat silently from time to time. Your first silent meal may cause you to feel a little uncomfortable, but once you become used to it, you will realize that meals in silence bring much peace and happiness. It is like turning off the TV before eating. We "turn off" the talking to enjoy the food and the presence of one another.

I do not recommend silent meals every day. I think talking to each other is a wonderful way to be in touch. But we have to distinguish among different kinds of talk. Some subjects can separate us, for instance if we talk about other people's shortcomings. The food that has been prepared carefully will have no value if we let this kind of talk dominate our meal. When instead we speak about things that nourish our awareness of the food and our being together, we cultivate the kind of happiness that is necessary for us to grow. If we compare this experience with the experience of talking about other people's shortcomings, I think awareness of a piece of bread in your mouth is a much more nourishing experience. It brings life in and makes life real.

I propose that during eating, you refrain from discussing subjects that can destroy the awareness of the family and the food. But you should feel free to say things that can nourish awareness and happiness. For instance, if there is a dish that you like very much, you can see if other people are also enjoying it, and if one of them is not, you can help them appreciate the wonderful dish prepared with loving care. If someone is thinking about something other than the good food on the table, such as their difficulties in the office or with friends, it means they are losing the present moment and the food. You can say,

"This dish is wonderful, don't you agree?" When you say something like this, you will draw them out of their thinking and worries and bring them back to the here and now, enjoying you, enjoying the wonderful dish. You become a bodhisattva, helping a living being become enlightened. I know that children, in particular, are very capable of practicing mindfulness and reminding others to do the same.

VERSES
FOR
DAILY
ACTIVITIES

40

TOUCHING THE EARTH

Earth brings us to life
and nourishes us.
Earth takes us back again.
We are born and we die with every breath.

The earth is our mother. All life arises from her and is nourished by her. Each of us is a child of the earth and, at some time, the earth will take us back to her again. In fact, we are continuously coming to life and returning to the bosom of the earth. We who practice meditation should be able to see birth and death in every breath.

Touching the earth, letting your fingers feel the soil, and gardening are wonderful restorative activities. If you live in a city, you may not have many opportunities to hoe the earth, plant vegetables, or take care of flowers. But you can still find and appreciate a small patch of grass or earth and care for it. Being in touch with Mother Earth is a wonderful way to preserve your mental health.

41

LOOKING AT YOUR HAND

Whose hand is this
that has never died?
Who is it who was born in the past?
Who is it who will die in the future?

If you look deeply into the palm of your hand, you will see your parents and all generations of your ancestors. All of them are alive in this moment. Each is present in your body. You are the continuation of each of these people.

To be born means that something that did not exist comes into existence. But the day we are "born" is not our beginning. It is a day of continuation. But that should not make us less happy when we celebrate our "Happy Continuation Day."

Since we are never born, how can we cease to be? This is what the Heart Sutra reveals to us. When we have a tangible experience of no birth and no death, we know ourselves beyond duality. The meditation on "no separate self" is one way to pass through the gate of birth and death.

Your hand proves that you have never been born and you will never die. The thread of life has never been interrupted from time without beginning until now.

Previous generations, all the way back to single-celled beings, are present in your hand at this moment. You can observe and experience this. Your hand is always available as a subject for meditation.

42

GOING UP AND DOWN STAIRS

Going up or down the stairs,
I keep my steps light.
If I hear my shoes click-clack,
I know my mind's not at peace.

We can make the staircase a place of special practice for mindful walking. If we notice that we are walking up or down unmindfully, we go back down or up again (mindfully) and start all over again. This may seem a little tedious, but it is a good way of training ourselves to walk mindfully. Once we can walk mindfully up and down stairs, we shall be able to do the same everywhere. The noise that our footsteps make serves as a bell of mindfulness telling us about our state of mind.

43

HEARING THE BELL

Listen, listen,
this wonderful sound
brings me back
to my true self.

Listening to the bell, our mind becomes one with the sound as it vibrates along, settles down, and fades away. With the help of a bell, our mind is collected and brought back to the present moment. The bell of mindfulness is the voice of the Buddha calling us back to ourselves. We have to respect each sound, stop our thinking and talking, and get in touch with ourselves, breathing and smiling. This is not a Buddha from the outside. It is our own Buddha calling us home.

If we cannot hear the sound of the bell, then we cannot hear other sounds that also come from the Buddha—the whistling of the wind, the songs of the birds, the cries of a baby, or even the motors of cars passing by. We can also hear the music of the bell in the ring of the doorbell or the telephone. These are all calls from the Buddha, reminding us to return to our "true selves."

What is a "true self?" A true self is a self that is made of nonself elements. If we are able to look in this way, the word "self" will no longer be a source of confusion. Practicing with a bell helps us practice conscious breathing and realize the interdependent nature of all existence.

44

USING THE TELEPHONE

Words can travel thousands of miles.
May my words create mutual understanding and love.
May they be as beautiful as gems,
as lovely as flowers.

The telephone is a very convenient means of communication. It can save us travel time and expense. But the telephone can also tyrannize us. If it is always ringing, we are disturbed and cannot accomplish much. If we talk on the phone without awareness, we waste precious time and money. Often we say things that are not important. How many times have we received our telephone bill and winced at the amount that is due!

When the telephone rings, the bell creates in us a kind of vibration, maybe some anxiety: "Who is calling? Is it good news or bad news?" There is a force that pulls us to the phone. We cannot resist. We are victims of our own telephone.

The next time you hear the phone ring, I recommend you stay exactly where you are, and become aware of your breathing: "Breathing in, I calm my body. Breathing out, I smile." When the phone rings the second time, you can breathe again. I am sure that this time your smile will be more solid than before. When it rings the third time, you can continue practicing breathing, while moving slowly to the phone. Remember, you are your own master, walking like a Buddha to the phone, dwelling in mindfulness. When you pick up the phone, you know that you are smiling, not only for your own sake but also for the sake of the other person. If you are irritated or angry, the other person will receive your negativity. But since you are smiling, how fortunate for them!

Before you make a phone call, I suggest you breathe in and out twice, and recite the four lines of this verse. Then pick up the phone and dial. When the bell rings, you know that your friend is breathing and smiling and will not pick up the phone until the third ring. So you continue to practice: "Breathing in, I calm my body. Breathing out, I smile." Both of you are close to your phones, breathing and smiling. This is very beautiful! You don't have to go into a meditation hall to do this wonderful practice. It is available in your house or office. Practicing telephone meditation can counteract stress and depression and bring the Buddha into your daily life.

We should not underestimate the effect our words have when we use right speech. The words we speak can build up understanding and love. They can be as beautiful as gems, as lovely as flowers, and they can make many people happy. The telephone gatha can help us practice right speech, and it can also help us keep our phone bills down.

45

TURNING ON THE TELEVISION

The mind is a television
with thousands of channels.
I choose a world that is tranquil and calm
so that my joy will always be fresh.

Our mind is like a television set with thousands of channels, and the channel we switch on is the channel we *are* at that moment. When we turn on anger, we are anger. When we turn on peace and joy, we are peace and joy. We have the ability to select the channel. We are what we choose to be. We can select any channel of the mind. Buddha is a channel, Mara is a channel, remembering is a channel, forgetting is a channel, calm is a channel, agitation is a channel. Changing from one state of being to another is as simple as the change from a channel showing a film to a channel playing music.

There are people who cannot tolerate peace and quiet, who are afraid of facing themselves, so they turn on the television in order to be preoccupied with it for a whole evening. But meditating can be just as entertaining, and you may find a whole evening has passed!

46

TURNING ON THE COMPUTER

Turning on the computer,
my mind gets in touch with the store.
I vow to transform habit energies
to help love and understanding grow.

Sometimes, when we are on the computer, it is as if we have turned off our mind and are absorbed into the computer for hours. Mind is consciousness. The two aspects of consciousness, subject and object, depend on each other to exist. When our mind is conscious of something, we are that thing. When we contemplate a snow-covered mountain, we are that mountain. When we watch a noisy film, we are that noisy film. And when we turn on the blue light of the computer, we become that computer.

The "store" in this verse refers to *alayavijñana*, the consciousness where all our seed-potentials are stored. We receive seeds from our ancestors, friends, and society; and they are held in our consciousness, just as the earth holds the seeds that fall upon it. Like the seeds in the earth, the seeds in our store consciousness are hidden from us; we are seldom in contact with them. Our store consciousness has a strong capacity to receive and absorb impressions, and this affects our patterns of seeing, feeling, and behaving. We interpret everything we see or hear in terms of our habit energy. If you crumple a sheet of paper, it is difficult to make it lie flat again. It has the habit energy of being crumpled. We are the same. The good news is that we can change our habit energies.

When using the computer, we practice mindfulness. Before turning the computer on, recite the gatha. It's possible to program your computer to make the sound of the bell every fifteen minutes so you can stop, breathe, smile, bring body and mind together, and release any tension in your shoulders or hands. If you are working for a longer period, you may want to get up occasionally and take some steps around the room to refresh yourself and help your circulation. Always type and read in a relaxed way, taking breaks to look out the window to rest your eyes.

The Buddha said that the eyes are a deep ocean with hidden waves and sea monsters beneath. If you are not mindful and do not know how to protect and guard the doors of your senses, you will be drowned in the ocean of forms, sometimes several times a day. With the boat of mindfulness, we sail across the ocean of forms, sounds, and other sense objects; and we hold on tight. Our boat does not sink, and we do not drown in the ocean of the senses.

47

CLEANING THE BATHROOM

How wonderful it is
to scrub and clean.
Day by day,
the heart and mind grow clearer.

Most of us do not like cleaning the bathroom. But when we work in full awareness of the present moment, we can find purity in each act. To purify means to become clear and calm. Cleaning the bathroom, we clear and purify our environment and ourselves.

In centers for meditation practice, often there is a vase of flowers in every bathroom. The bathroom is as important a place as the meditation hall for practicing mindfulness. In fact, the bathroom is another meditation hall, and so we offer a vase of flowers there. Flowers arranged with skill and care remind us that we can live in such a way that we clarify and calm our hearts and minds. I hope you will put a vase of flowers in your bathroom at home.

48

SWEEPING

As I carefully sweep
the ground of enlightenment,
a tree of understanding
springs up from the earth.

This gatha is based on two lines of Chinese poetry: "Sweeping the floor of the monastery, the benefits of understanding are realized." The whole earth is the land of the Buddha. The path around our home is also the ground of awakening. It is said that Mara, a spirit who represents delusion, offered the Buddha a parcel of land as large as the Buddha's robe could cover. But when the Buddha's robe flew up to the sky, it covered the entire earth with its shadow. So we say that the earth on which we stand, the earth in front of our house, and the earth that we cultivate, all belong to the Buddha. In Vietnam, at the New Year, we put a pole topped by the Buddhist flag in front of our house to remind Mara how far Buddha's land extends—and to keep Mara out!

Any ground we sweep in full awareness is the ground of enlightenment. True mindfulness always gives rise to awakened understanding.

49

WATERING THE GARDEN

Sunshine and water
make plants fresh and green.
When the rain of compassion falls,
even the desert becomes a vast fertile plain.

Water is the balm of compassion. It has the capacity to restore us to life. The Bodhisattva of Compassion is often depicted holding a vase of water in her left hand and a willow branch in her right. She sprinkles down com passion, like drops of nurturing water, to revitalize tired hearts and minds weak from suffering. Rain enlivens crops and protects people from hunger. Watering the garden, the compassionate rain falls on the plants. Our respect and gratitude for this gift of water helps us heal ourselves and transform even a desert into a vast fertile plain.

When we offer water to plants, we offer it to the whole earth. When watering plants, if we speak to them, we are also speaking to ourselves. We exist in relationship to all other phenomena. As we water plants, we can speak to them:

Dear plant, you are not alone.
This stream of water comes from earth and sky.
We are together for innumerable lifetimes.

The feeling of alienation among so many people today has come about because they lack awareness of the inter-connectedness of all things. We cannot separate ourselves from society or anything else. "This is like this because that is like that" is a phrase taken from the sutras, summarizing the principle of interrelatedness. To water plants and experience compassion and interconnectedness is a wonderful practice of meditation.

50

PLANTINGS

I entrust myself to Earth;
Earth entrusts herself to me.
I entrust myself to Buddha;
Buddha entrusts herself to me.

To plant a seed or a seedling is to entrust it to the earth. The plant takes refuge in the earth. Whether the plant grows well or not depends on the earth. Many generations of vegetation have grown bright and beautiful under the light of the sun to create fertile topsoil. This topsoil will continue to nourish generations of vegetation to come. Whether the earth is beautiful, fresh, and green, or withered and dry depends on the plants entrusted to the earth. The plants and the earth rely on each other for life.

When we entrust ourselves to the Buddha, we take refuge in the essence of nourishment, the soil of enlightened understanding, love, and compassion. And the Buddha also entrusts herself to us, because awakened understanding, love, and compassion need each of us in order to germinate and flourish. How can these attributes continue to flower in the world if we do not realize them within ourselves? "I entrust myself to the Buddha" is what we usually think, but let us also notice that Buddha is entrusting herself to become real within us, just as the earth and the green plants entrust themselves to one another.

51

PICKING A FLOWER

May I pick you, little flower,
gift of earth and sky?
Thank you, dear bodhisattva,
for making life beautiful.

Whenever we pick a flower, we can ask permission, not only of the plant, but of the earth and sky as well. The whole earth and sky joined to create this flower. Our gratitude to them must be sincere. A flower is a bodhisattva that makes life fresher and more beautiful. We, too, can offer others a gift by being refreshing, compassionate, and happy.

There is a well-known story in Zen circles about a flower. One day the Buddha was holding up a flower in front of an audience of 1,250 monks and nuns. He did not say anything for a long time. A man in the audience, named Mahakashyapa, smiled at him and at the flower. The Buddha smiled back and said, "I have a treasure of insight, and I have transmitted it to Mahakashyapa." To me the meaning is quite simple: be in touch with life in the present moment and look deeply into things that happen in the present moment. The person who was not thinking, who was just himself, encountered the flower in depth and smiled.

52

ARRANGING FLOWERS

Arranging this flower
in the saha world,
the ground of my mind
is pure and calm.

The saha world, according to Buddhist mythology, is the planet Earth, the "ground" for enduring hardships, sickness, hatred, ignorance, and war. Saha means "moving" and "enduring." When we practice the teachings of the Buddha, we transform ourselves and set up a beautiful pure land, full of miraculous wonders, here on Earth.

Arranging flowers is something we can do to help make life more beautiful. When we are mindful while arranging flowers, not only the flowers become beautiful, but we become beautiful as well. When our heart's garden is calm and radiant, and the flowers of our heart light the way, people around us will recognize the beauty of life and realize how precious it is to be alive.

53

SMILING TO YOUR ANGER

Breathing in, I feel my anger.
Breathing out, I smile.
I stay with my breathing
so I won't lose myself.

When we feel angry, we should go back to our conscious breathing and refrain from looking and listening to the person we think to be the source of our unhappiness. We do not need to do or say anything. As we go back to our breathing and breathe according to the gatha, we should be aware that it's our anger that is making us suffer, not the other person.

Taking the first breath and reciting the first line of the gatha is like looking at ourselves in a mirror. As we see ourselves clearly, we know what to do and what not to do. The exhalation that follows will have the same effect. In anger, we tend to think of the other person as the source of our suffering. We see evil in them. "They are cruel." "They oppress me." "They want to destroy me!" In fact, it is our anger that destroys us.

So we must take good care of our anger. When a house is burning, we must first go into the house and try to put out the fire. It is too soon to go searching for the person who may have started the fire. That is what we see in the inhalation that goes with the third line of the gatha. When we exhale, we recite the last line. Only loving kindness can take care of our anger, and only loving kindness can take care of the other person.

54

WASHING FEET

The peace and joy
of one toe
is peace and joy
for my whole body.

We take our toes for granted. We worry about so many things, but we seldom think about our toes. If one small toe steps on a thorn, however, our whole body will feel the pain. Holding one toe in our hand, we can feel its peace and joy. It has been a good friend. It is not broken. It does not have cancer. We can thank our toe for its health and well-being.

Our toe and each cell of our body exist interdependently, not separately. If our body becomes ill or injured, the cause may be external, such as bacteria from contaminated food, alcohol in another driver's bloodstream, or a bomb dropped from a plane. If the sun were to stop shining, life on Earth would cease. We must understand that our body also includes all of these things. The sun is our heart outside of our body. Our life and the life of all existence are one continuous life. The peace and joy of our small toe are the peace and joy of our whole body and mind, and the peace and joy of the entire universe. Once we identify with our toe, we can proceed further to identify ourselves with all life. Life comes from the whole universe. When we identify with the life of all that exists, we realize that birth and death are minor fluctuations in an ever-changing cosmos.

55

DRIVING THE CAR

Before starting the car,
I know where I am going.
The car and I are one.
If the car goes fast, I go fast.

If we are mindful when we start our car, we will know how to use it properly. When we are driving, we tend to think of arriving, and we sacrifice the journey for the sake of the arrival. But life is to be found in the present moment, not in the future. In fact, we may suffer more after we arrive at our destination. If we have to talk of a destination, what about our final destination, the graveyard? We don't want to go in the direction of death; we want to go to in the direction of life. Life can be found only in the present moment. Therefore, each mile we drive, each step we take, has to bring us into the present moment.

When we see a red light or a stop sign, we can smile at it and thank it, because it is a bodhisattva helping us return to the present moment. The red light is a bell of mindfulness. We may have thought of it as an enemy, preventing us from achieving our goal. But now we know the red light is our friend, helping us resist rushing and calling us to return to the present moment where we can meet with life, joy, and peace.

The next time you are caught in traffic, don't fight. It is useless to fight. If you sit back and smile to yourself, you will enjoy the present moment and make everyone in the car happy. The Buddha is there because the Buddha can always be found in the present moment. Practicing meditation is to return to the present moment in order to encounter the flower, the blue sky, the child, the brilliant red light.

56

RECYCLING

In the garbage, I see a rose.
In the rose, I see the garbage.
Everything is in transformation.
Even permanence is impermanent.

Whenever we throw something away, whether in the garbage can, the compost, or the recycling, it can smell terrible. Rotting organic matter smells especially terrible. But it can also become rich compost for fertilizing the garden. The fragrant rose and the stinking garbage are two sides of the same existence. Without one, the other cannot be. Everything is in transformation. The rose that wilts after six days will become a part of the garbage. After six months the garbage is transformed into a rose. When we speak of impermanence, we understand that everything is in transformation. This becomes that, and that becomes this.

Looking deeply, we can contemplate one thing and see everything else in it. We are not disturbed by change when we see the interconnectedness and continuity of all things. It is not that the life of any individual is permanent but that life itself continues. When we identify ourselves with life and go beyond the boundaries of a separate identity, we shall be able to see permanence in the impermanent, or the rose in the garbage.

57

HUGGING MEDITATION

Breathing in,
I am so happy to hug my beloved.
Breathing out,
I know they are real and alive in my arms.

Suppose a lovely child comes and presents themself to us. If we are not really there—if we are thinking of the past, worrying about the future, or possessed by anger or fear—the child, although present, will not exist for us. They are like a ghost, and we are like a ghost also. If we want to meet the child, we have to go back to the present moment in order to meet them. If we want to hug them, it is only in the present moment that we can hug them.

So we breathe consciously, uniting body and mind, making ourselves into a real person again. When we become a real person, the child becomes real also. They are a wondrous presence. If we hold them in our arms and continue to breathe, we will feel truly alive. This gatha can help us remember the preciousness of our loved one as we hold them in our arms.

58

ENDING THE DAY

The day is ending,
our life is one day shorter.
Let us look carefully
at what we have done.
Let us practice diligently,
putting our whole heart into the path of meditation.
Let us live deeply each moment in freedom,
so time does not slip away meaninglessly.

We can practice beginning anew at any moment of our life. To be born is to begin anew. When you are three years old, you can begin anew; when you are sixty years old, you can begin anew; and when you are about to die, that is still a time to begin anew. When we look deeply, we see that beginning anew is possible at any time of our daily life, at any age.

As humans, we make mistakes. Without these mistakes, there would be no way to learn to be more accepting and compassionate. We should not get caught in the prison of guilt. If we can learn from our mistakes, then we have already begun transforming garbage into flowers. It is always possible for us to begin anew so that our life is filled with meaning. When your life is meaningful, happiness becomes a reality, and you become a bodhisattva right here and now. A bodhisattva is someone who has compassion within themselves and who is able to make another person smile or help someone suffer less. Every one of us is capable of this.

VERSES
FOR
ENTERING
THE
ULTIMATE
DIMENSION

Poetry comes from deep levels of consciousness in the poet. We call that consciousness "store" because it contains the seeds of all that is possible. The seeds of enlightenment and liberation are all available in store. Store is individual but it is also collective. These verses on the ultimate and historical dimensions are to help us be in touch with the depths of love and understanding in our own consciousness. If the verse has the words "in the ultimate dimension" in the first line, it is an invitation to step into that dimension straightaway; that is the realm of no birth and no death, no being and no nonbeing. If the verse has the words "the historical dimension" in the first line, it is an invitation to go deeply into the historical to touch the ultimate.

59

URINATING

Urinating in the ultimate dimension,
a wonderful exchange happens.
I and you are not two.
No loss and no gain.

This verse helps us to look at the water cycle in nature. Water has come into our body and flows throughout our body and then leaves in the form of urine, perspiration, tears, etc. You see that in this exchange water inside your body and water outside are just one water cycling in nature. This will help you to realize the meaning of "I and you are not two"; water inside we call I, and water outside we call you, but really they are not two.

60

PUTTING ON CLOTHES

Putting on clothes in the historical dimension,
I adorn myself and the world.
The pure land is in the palm of my hand,
created by mountains and rivers together.

In the Buddhist teachings there are two kinds of retribution or fruits of action. The first is our body and mind; the second is our environment. When we put on our clothes, we contemplate that we are making our person beautiful and making our environment beautiful. We adorn ourselves with the practice of the Five Mindfulness Trainings—the Buddhist vision for a global spirituality and ethic—and at the same time we adorn our environment with understanding and love. The pure land is not something we realize when we die. It is available here and now in the beauties of nature, the mountains and rivers.

61

WALKING WITH YOUR FEET

In the ultimate dimension,
I walk with my feet and not with my head.
When I walk with my head,
I lose my way.

If we are thinking about the past or the future as we walk, we miss out on the wonders of life in the present moment. In order to touch the ultimate dimension, we need to be very alive in the here and the now. Each step helps us transcend our usual ideas of what is and what is not.

62

WALKING AND TOUCHING ETERNITY

Taking a stroll in the ultimate dimension,
your hand in my hand,
thousands of years before
and thousands of years after,
we return together to the path.

In the ultimate dimension you can hold the hand of someone who is no longer there historically. It could be the hand of Shakyamuni Buddha, Jesus Christ, Martin Luther King, or any great being or friend you choose to walk with. When we walk in the ultimate dimension, we are not caught in ideas of past and future.

63

SITTING IN THE HISTORICAL DIMENSION

Sitting at leisure in the historical dimension,
I lean against a boulder.
That butterfly is still there.
This rose is no stranger.

Sitting in nature at the seaside or on a bank of grass in the mountains, you can be in touch deeply with the historical dimension. You look at the butterfly and recognize that it is a wonderful manifestation. A butterfly does not live long, but it seems to enjoy every moment of its short life, going from flower to flower. The rose is a friend with whom you have been intimately connected for a very long time.

We human beings need to learn again how to sit at leisure. Do not just do things! Please just sit there!

64

SITTING WITH ANXIETY

Sitting at leisure in the historical dimension,
if I hear my anxiety bubbling,
I look at the ultimate and smile.
The three times interpenetrate freely.

When we sit at leisure, anxiety might suddenly come up in us. Usually when these unpleasant feelings manifest, we will do something to try and cover them up. We could go to the refrigerator to find something to eat, turn on the television, pick up the telephone or a magazine or book. This verse reminds us to do differently: we remain seated to listen to our self deeply. We can recognize how past, present, and future inter-are, and the most important thing is how we are in the present. That determines how the future will be. So we have nothing more to be anxious about. The smile is important. It sends a message of hope to our brain.

65

WEEDING

Weeding in the ultimate dimension,
I remember when I was a child.
May all children
be safe and free from fear.

Weeding is something that all gardeners have to do from time to time. At first, we may feel that it is a little bit destructive. Still, we can do it with a heart of love and compassion. When you were a child, you were fresh, innocent, and shy. That child weeding the garden is still there in the ultimate dimension. You feel love for the child that was yourself, and at the same time you feel love for all children.

66

RAKING LEAVES

Raking leaves in the ultimate dimension,
each leaf is a wonderful manifestation.
In the game of hide-and-seek,
there is no coming and no going.

In the autumn millions of leaves find their way gracefully back to the earth. They are playing a game of hide-and-seek. In the spring, they manifested as a young bud; in the summer, as a bright green leaf nourishing the tree with sunshine and air; in the autumn, as a yellow or red leaf lying on the earth, in the winter, decomposing to become one with the earth to nourish the tree again. All these manifestations show how the leaf is never born and never dies.

67

WASHING DISHES

Washing dishes in the historical dimension,
I smile to myself.
What am I doing?
Over there a fresh rosebud opens.

Because I am in the historical dimension, I may not be very mindful. Then I recognize this, and I stop and ask myself what I am doing. I tell myself: "I am washing the dishes." Then I ask another question: "Why am I doing it?" The answer is not "In order to have clean dishes," because dishes will never remain clean. The answer will be "I am washing dishes to touch peace and joy in the present moment," or "I am washing dishes to express my love for my family or community." This brings me back to the present moment, and in my heart there is a fresh rosebud. Sometimes a Zen master comes into the kitchen and asks you what you are doing. If, while washing the dishes, you answer the master: "I am washing dishes," they will be very disappointed. They can see perfectly well that you are washing dishes. They need you to tell them about your state of mind. If it is as fresh as a rosebud, they will be happy for you.

68

WASHING DISHES IN FREEDOM

Washing dishes in the historical dimension,
I see them piled high.
Looking from the ultimate dimension,
I am happy washing dishes forever.

When you see a huge pile of dishes, you may feel a little daunted. If you know how to wash dishes in mindfulness,* each dish becomes a precious occasion for enlightenment. Normally we want to finish washing the dishes so we can go on to what we consider a more worthwhile activity. In the ultimate dimension no activity is more worthwhile than what we are doing in the present moment.

---

* For more on basic mindfulness practice, see Thich Nhat Hanh, *The Miracle of Mindfulness* (Boston MA: Beacon Press, 1999).

69

SHARING THE DHARMA

Sharing the Dharma in the ultimate dimension,
I look at you and smile.
Yes, you are me.
The listener and the speaker are one and the same.

We gather in groups from time to time to share our experience of our spiritual practice. The fact that we can share depends on the fact that there is someone who listens. If there were no one there to listen, how could we share? With that in mind, you will speak in a way that is beneficial for the hearer. You will look at the listener and feel the effect your words are having.

70

EATING WITH ANCESTORS AND DESCENDANTS

Eating in the historical dimension,
I nourish all my ancestors.
I open a way for my descendants,
and together we can find a beautiful path forward.

When we see that we and our ancestors and descendants are one, we begin to go into the ultimate dimension. We are part of a stream of life with all of them. Our father, mother, and grandparents all live on in us, and whenever we eat, they eat with us. This kind of awareness means that we are mindful of what we eat. We realize that this body is not just ours to do what we like with. We have received a precious inheritance, and we want to take care of it for the future generations. Our descendants are our future, and whatever we do in our daily life can nourish them or harm them.

71

EATING WITH COMPASSION

Eating in the historical dimension,
my chewing is as rhythmic as my breathing.
How miraculously we nourish each other.
May I maintain compassion alive
and help all beings to the other shore.

It is wonderful that we nourish each other, but it can also be dreadful. The lion has to eat the deer, the bird the insect, the snake the frog. As human beings, we do not have to eat other animals; we can follow a vegan diet. If we look deeply into our vegan diet, we shall see that other living beings have lost their lives because of the cultivation of our vegetables and grains. Seeing this we are determined to eat in such a way that keeps our compassion alive. We nourish our compassion by eating in a way that causes as little suffering as possible, although we know that by eating, we will cause some beings to suffer.

72

BEING ANGRY

Angry with someone in the historical dimension,
*   I breathe.*
I look at the ultimate and smile.
Love and hatred take turns in the game
like the rising and falling of river waters.

Love and hatred are organic. We can quickly become angry with the one we love, and we can also come to love someone we hated formerly. When we are angry, we can give ourselves a little space by taking some deep breaths. This will prevent us from saying or doing something that we may regret later. We recognize that this feeling of anger is a momentary reaction. If we do not feed it with the way we perceive, it will cease.

73

THE IMPERMANENCE
OF ANGER

Feeling angry in the historical dimension,
I close my eyes and look into the future.
Three hundred years from now
where you will be and where shall I be?

This verse helps you have enough presence of mind to close your eyes and not look at the person who is making you angry. Breathing mindfully with your eyes closed, you bring your mind to the distant future. Your body and the body of the person with whom you are angry will have dissolved into dust. When we see our life is so ephemeral, we do not want to waste our time being angry with each other.

74

RESTING

Resting in the ultimate dimension,
the snow-capped mountains are my pillow.
With arms embracing the pink clouds,
I become the never-ending mountains and rolling hills.

There may be moments during the day when you lie down to take a short rest. If you touch the ultimate dimension, you will see that you are not limited by your body and the mat on which you are lying. Your mind becomes very spacious, embracing earth and sky.

75

TAKING OUT THE COMPOST

Taking out the compost in the ultimate dimension,
I look with nondualistic eyes.
Entrusting the compost to the future,
flowers blossom in the next century.

We have the tendency to discriminate between clean and unclean. We see the flower as clean and the compost as unclean. In the ultimate dimension there is no discrimination between pure and impure. We can already see the flower that is waiting to be born from the compost. This verse also reminds us to be aware of the rubbish that we produce. If we continue to fill our earth and oceans with plastic, flowers will not be able to grow on this planet. We want to consume mindfully and not produce the kind of rubbish that cannot be recycled by nature.

76

LONELY

Feeling lonely in the historical dimension,
I embrace my pain
with a gentle lullaby,
like falling snowflakes covering the whole mountain.

We all feel lonely from time to time. We should not try to cover up our loneliness. Rather we recognize it and gently take care of it as a mother or father takes care of a crying baby. We continue to take care in this way until we feel the loneliness begin to transform.

77

SITTING MEDITATION

Sitting in the historical dimension
anywhere can be a place of enlightenment.
Through countless rounds of birth and death,
this moment is unique.

Anywhere we sit in mindfulness can be a place where we can realize a small enlightenment and liberate ourselves from some form of bondage. Enlightenment does not have to be a major enlightenment; it can come in stages as more and more small enlightenments accumulate. We have been through countless rounds of birth and death, but each moment is unique and deserves our full attention.

78

WATERING THE GARDEN

As I water the garden in the ultimate dimension,
I am part of life.
Clouds and snow are in this stream of water
as they go from high mountains to the wide ocean.

Watering the garden is a chance for us to see that we can make a wholesome contribution to life. We can give a helping hand to the trees, flowers, shrubs, and vegetation that are essential for human beings. We stand in awe before the water cycle.

79

MENDING MY CLOTHES

Mending clothes in the historical dimension,
I am making my life whole again.
With needle and thread,
I realize fruits of the practice.

There is a story of a practitioner who realized the fruit of awakening while making six stitches as he mended his robe. As we sit peacefully and mend our clothes, we can see in our hands our ancestors who sat peacefully in the evening mending clothes. To be able to sit peacefully, wholly concentrated on the sewing, and to have the insight that these hands are the hands of my ancestors, are fruits of the practice.

Monastics and visitors practice the art of mindful living in the tradition of Thich Nhat Hanh at our mindfulness practice centers around the world. To reach any of these communities, or for information about how individuals, couples, and families can join in a retreat, please contact:

PLUM VILLAGE
33580 Dieulivol, France
plumvillage.org

LA MAISON DE L'INSPIR
77510 Villeneuve-sur-Bellot, France
maisondelinspir.org

HEALING SPRING
MONASTERY
77510 Verdelot, France
healingspringmonastery.org

MAGNOLIA GROVE
MONASTERY
Batesville, MS 38606, USA
magnoliagrovemonastery.org

BLUE CLIFF MONASTERY
Pine Bush, NY 12566, USA
bluecliffmonastery.org

DEER PARK MONASTERY
Escondido, CA 92026, USA
deerparkmonastery.org

EUROPEAN INSTITUTE OF
APPLIED BUDDHISM
D-51545 Waldbröl, Germany
eiab.eu

THAILAND PLUM VILLAGE
Nakhon Ratchasima
30130 Thailand
thaiplumvillage.org

ASIAN INSTITUTE OF
APPLIED BUDDHISM
Lantau Island, Hong Kong
pvfhk.org

STREAM ENTERING
MONASTERY
Beaufort, Victoria 3373
Australia
nhapluu.org

MOUNTAIN SPRING
MONASTERY
Bilpin, NSW 2758, Australia
mountainspringmonastery.org

For more information visit: plumvillage.org
To find an online sangha visit: plumline.org
For more resources, try the Plum Village app: plumvillage.app
Social media: @thichnhathanh @plumvillagefrance

THICH NHAT HANH FOUNDATION

planting seeds of Compassion

THE THICH NHAT HANH FOUNDATION works to continue the mindful teachings and practice of Zen Master Thich Nhat Hanh, in order to foster peace and transform suffering in all people, animals, plants, and our planet. Through donations to the Foundation, thousands of generous supporters ensure the continuation of Plum Village practice centers and monastics around the world, bring transformative practices to those who otherwise would not be able to access them, support local mindfulness initiatives, and bring humanitarian relief to communities in crisis in Vietnam.

By becoming a supporter, you join many others who want to learn and share these life-changing practices of mindfulness, loving speech, deep listening, and compassion for oneself, each other, and the planet.

For more information on how you can help support mindfulness around the world, or to subscribe to the Foundation's monthly newsletter with teachings, news, and global retreats, visit tnhf.org.

THE MINDFULNESS BELL, a Journal of the Art of Mindful Living in the Tradition of Thich Nhat Hanh, is published two times a year by Plum Village. To subscribe or to see the worldwide directory of Sanghas, visit **www.mindfulnessbell.org**.